PRAISE FOR LAURA DA'

"In *Severalty*, Laura Da' has rendered an unimaginably brilliant creation. She achieves the furthest reaches of the lyric's capacity for resurrective stitchery, restoring the quartered body to wholeness and the land to paradise. This is a holy text, with the power to reveal and heal. I am in awe."

—DIANE SEUSS, author of *Modern Poetry* and *frank: sonnets*

"The growing oeuvre from Laura Da' continues to astonish. With *Severalty*, she casts her 'earth-slung eye' to the deep roots of Indigenous history, culture, and identity. These pages are scarred with violence, allotment, and surgery. At the same time, these poems cast and stitch seeds, offering medicine and sustenance."

—CRAIG SANTOS PEREZ, author of *from unincorporated territory [åmot]*

"In this riveting new collection, Laura Da' braids the Shawnee history of allotment with personal history, and her 'stitches are as many' and as various 'as any primer.' Here 'Q is the needle's threaded eye' and 'Z . . . a tight flourish across the page, precarious ink edge of survival.'"

—ARTHUR SZE, author of *Sight Lines*

"In *Severalty*, Laura Da' is transfixed by the hidden history of our Native landscape. She has a huge armory of voices to draw upon to realize this vision. Her poetry is so exacting and vibrant as to transfigure time. She seems to escape its restraints again and again. Her deftly arranged serial poems maintain the presence and precise weight of sculpture. Are these poems in fact ceremonial objects? A fully attenuated and syllabic rendering of 'nature' is being offered here. This book is a multidimensional act of reclamation."

—CEDAR SIGO, author of *Siren of Atlantis*

"Though the title of this haunting collection alludes to the act of separating—Native communal land holdings, the continuum of time—the poems 'ripen outside the hours and beyond the map.' Here, history and family stories overlap; here historical trauma leads to contemporary illness. Ultimately, Da' employs the Shawnee understanding of the verb *garden* as 'tenderly rupturing,' to enact an alchemy in which the reader, like the author, may be 'tilled by memory / . . . sown and cultivated / back from the brink.' Read these poems, let the 'untranslatable' seeds fill you."

—KIMBERLY BLAESER, author of *Ancient Light*

"In *Severalty*, Laura Da' brilliantly explores territorial, historical, and personal notions of separation. The poems in this insightful, candid, and revelatory collection weave the present and the past, the personal and the political, and the legal and the communal into a stunning poetic tapestry. This is a book of visions, interrogations, memory, hope, and guidance. It is a necessary book."

—DEAN RADER, author of *Self-Portrait as Wikipedia Entry*

"Laura Da' dives yet more deeply to examine body, land, community over time, contrasting perspectives from classical Western culture with her Shawnee world. Vulnerable after general anesthesia, Da' returns to Self 'Mistaken for a gardener upon my return' that leads her to ponder resurrection and what is essential. She conjures her people's journey downriver from Chillicothe to Oklahoma and back to the Snoqualmie Valley watershed through interlocking poems that analyze erasure, even as they celebrate life. The sharp, apt images that surface will take your breath again and again."

—RUBY HANSEN MURRAY, *Osage News*

SEVERALTY

LAURA DA'

SEVERALTY

POEMS

THE UNIVERSITY OF
ARIZONA PRESS
TUCSON

The University of Arizona Press
www.uapress.arizona.edu

We respectfully acknowledge the University of Arizona is on the land and territories of
Indigenous peoples. Today, Arizona is home to twenty-two federally recognized tribes, with
Tucson being home to the O'odham and the Yaqui. Committed to diversity and inclusion,
the University strives to build sustainable relationships with sovereign Native Nations and
Indigenous communities through education offerings, partnerships, and community service.

ISBN-13: 978-0-8165-5459-1 (paperback)
ISBN-13: 978-0-8165-5460-7 (ebook)

Cover design by Leigh McDonald
Cover art by Jarrod Da'
Designed and typeset by Leigh McDonald in Calluna 9.5/14 and Brother 1816 (display)

Publication of this book is made possible in part by the proceeds of a permanent endowment
created with the assistance of a Challenge Grant from the National Endowment for the
Humanities, a federal agency.

Library of Congress Cataloging-in-Publication Data
Names: Da', Laura, author.
Title: Severalty : poems / Laura Da'.
Description: Tucson : University of Arizona Press, 2025. | Series: Sun tracks ; volume 98
Identifiers: LCCN 2024038848 (print) | LCCN 2024038849 (ebook) | ISBN 9780816554591
    (paperback) | ISBN 9780816554607 (ebook)
Subjects: LCGFT: Poetry.
Classification: LCC PS3604.A16 S48 2025 (print) | LCC PS3604.A16 (ebook) | DDC
    811/.6—dc23/eng/20240826
LC record available at https://lccn.loc.gov/2024038848
LC ebook record available at https://lccn.loc.gov/2024038849

Printed in the United States of America
♾ This paper meets the requirements of ANSI/NISO Z39.48-1992 (Permanence of Paper).

CONTENTS

SEVERALTY

Mistaken for a gardener upon my return:
furrows in the story,

furrows in the soil. I clear a circular bed
for mounds of flint

corn and spokes of vining beans
in the counter aspect

of a clockface. When time is split
into a severalty,

who can resist lifting the green
lid of creation?

The shovel's splintering pole
harvests trinity

circles of deep light into
a cool, tapered path.

PAINTERLY

Classical viewpoint

      holds the world by the standing gaze.

High viewpoint
is the purview
of the elevated
and no concern of mine,

      holder of the wet brush

in the shaking hand,

      she of the earth-slung eye.

Look here,

behind the paint.

The tips of my fingers
buzzed and I had to be trussed up to standing

      from a slender bed.

Crosshatched,
the white and red
of a glass bead,
my mouth

catechized until sedated:

      Will I be remembered?

A nurse plotted
bleach-soaked
bandages on the side table,

one after another.

There was a fingernail view
of the slate-gray sound
around the IV pole.

I thought to fix
the image
of those slim waves

from my low perspective

if it was the last thing

I ever did.

TWELVE GATES

Strict and bound
as an analog watch,
Aristotelian narrative
calls for a probable
necessary sequence.

It is end-stage season.
The calendar taunts
with year three's death dance.

Dialysate swills
in my abdomen.
Long arrows of surgery
nudge under my ribs
        trace my hipbones
                garland my navel.

Along my lower back
divots of biopsy
freckle into sickles
when I bend over.

Driving over the city bridge
quirk or quark humming
        I might be spared.

My grandmother loved
singing *O! What a Beautiful City*
as she sorted her pills.

The anesthetic mask
shatters time's linear discipline:

Trotting the deep path by mosslight,
son is a dark-haired universe
in the crook of my right arm.

Five-pound blood hum,
prayer and verse ripping
my skull pure off.

Time has me scalped
kissing whorls of brain
with frank red lips.

Rolling up from surgery
I look down to my wrist
where someone has clasped
my watch on loosely.

THE LAZARUS STITCH

Pale birds of passage saddled
with the symbolism of rebirth

ride the greasy rivers
of the watershed
        in the fool's spring.

Resurrected, I wake and walk
wearing a new suit

for sun or rain,
sin or pain.

In Genesis:
sea, land, growing fruits—

back tacked
        in an ecstasy of conception
        to the world's frame.

From the womb
that quickens two nations,

        the first treaty is born.

On the other
side of the grass,

deep root systems
weave nests
        of consolation.

Dark lengths
of thread unspool

into human topography,
scrying green creation stories.

In the lazaretto,
eyes taped closed
like nascent jewels,

jaw cupped with reverence,
expert breaths

spool into the dark,

      questing favor.

Creators woo the throat
to hear the sounds—
waves from an old shore
      lapping against new land.

Poor Lazarus.

      Sleek alchemy

pivots the rock
of wakefulness.

Hagiographies rest
not; no mouth

asks any ancestor
      over the weeping

if the caved sleep,
devoid of murmurs of obligation,

is not a kind of paradise.

Ashen gates traverse the surface;
genesis stitches darn
deep, severing whole.

No matter how clean the healing—

a cave just under the skin.
A talon tucked in flight.

The beauty screen intercedes in the valley
of my hometown.

Which side is paradise and where
might a person

find just one of its twelve gates?
The clear-cut

unrobes an uncanny beauty. Emerald
ferns stretching

along the ropey brown earth
of deer trails

laid bare like the part line on a head
gone rapidly bald.

Certain slivers of vellum in sacred texts,
ruptured by the awl

of aging or the hand of the parchmenter,
are stitched closed

in bottle-green thread. The scars meander
like bean plants

creeping up the page in search of a strut
to grow against.

WATCH FACE

I.

Dowsing the rain crow,
I walked late of old habit.

Blackstrap molasses
night strolls—sweet
with a bite of bone
marrow at the center.

I was chasing upmountain,
out hunting the margins—

Scarce Creek
absconding down
the north face of Si,
where I once sniffed
a sorrel colt's birth drop.

The turquoise watch
I walked in wearing
swapped with garish
plastic bangles signaling
risk of fall and rejection.

2.

Playing the dozens
inside the canals
of my nerves, one hand
tapping out against
the safety rails
before fainting
like bailing off
a green broke horse
along rodeo arena rails.

I entreated flush walls:
        Where was my son?

Rappelling bedward
on the very lick
of midnight's leaving,
I reaped arrows
from the courage watch
ticking along
the perimeters
of my corneas.

3.

Escape wheels crenellated
the alarum mechanism at my navel
with clean new fangs.

I didn't have any say in all this,
but I begged for it. Let any ancestor
string me like an arrow then loose me
from exile's spit-soaked bow.

Where is the IV pole
so I might walk three
mincing circuits along
the twilight hallway?

Where is my benevolent
guide? Where is my call
button? Where is the buckskin vest traced
with my auntie's lazy-stitch hummingbirds?

4.

Bandages, pillows, then towels
braced against my guts. My joints
stove-up, crackling with scar tissue.

Who can I speak with
about bartering
back the minutes?

      I can't think about it now
      without my hands shaking.

5.

Battering my legs
back to rhythm,
my stride laid
phantom tines,
tracking a sharp o'clock.

I once walked miles
to see the intricacies
of a plaza clock
engraved with symbols
of the twelve-gated city,
so singular it apocryphally
cost the maker his dominant hand.

Exiled, skirting, probing
the ascetic territories
of eminent domain.

>Where is the heavenly city's weakest gate?
>Where is the clockmaker?
>Where is my cutting horse with the bright-white medicine hat?

6.

Slender silk cords
veiled inside the mechanism
compel table-clock automata
to dance, eat, converse, butcher,
kiss, swim, rape, harvest.

The cherub traces
the sun's peregrination—
fingers trailing zodiac symbols,
closing the day standing
above incised memento mori.

The running maiden
evades the galloping soldier
so long as the fingers wind.

SHAWNEE WORD FOR PRINCIPAL CITY

In the case of Chillicothe,
the city is contingent
on the river whose flow
is one of the four chambers
of the name. We leave

> Chillicothes at our heels.
> River homes ever

loading and unloading.
High banks to spare us deluge
nestle inside the word.
The principal city's devastation
froths beneath the flood;

> the many-faced
> town destroyers allot

our city into severalty.
Maps scuttle east
detailing imaginary cities
and singing papery hymns
to call down the torrents.

> Chillicothes water
> from the Piqua, the Scioto,

sip from Paint Creek,
from the lost meanders:
Grand, Wanders, Slip, and Red.
Chillicothe is engraved
on the tablet as first

capital city. In laments
it is the lost capital city

of our dominion;
the word *city* called
into existence, already existing,
carved on the gates of the city,
carved under the city

in the ash-charred lodges
by the survivors of the flood.

THE RHETORICAL FEMININE

Gliding from the confluence of Battery Rock
to the Devil's Backbone inside the Shawnee

National Forest makes a sound I cannot
duplicate in English. With one finger tracing

the route on an atlas, my tongue wet
with nostalgia—a waterlogged migration

by touch. I seek the cities without the words.
As late as somebody's 1810 there were headwater

communities of women for the express purpose of healing,
birthing, governing shared territory—crouched

in the frog-legged stance of delivery and defense.
Linguistic evidence suggests a pattern of feminization

in Shawnee rhetoric. *Nation of women,*
bellowed strangers even as river city

dialects mouthed spells that cured war like hides
and curved breech births veiled in water

to the banks of living territory. Gliding from the confluence
of Battery Rock to the Devil's Backbone

inside the Shawnee National Forest
makes a sound I cannot duplicate in English.

$\longrightarrow$

To say *garden* in Shawnee, one must
describe tenderly

rupturing the skin of the land. To spear
outside the constraints

of violence or wounding. The verb
is inherently communal

and perpetual. Bottle-green larvae hang
like earrings

from the far branches of an established oak.
Should an inchworm

fall to my shoulder, it measures the stitches
of my funeral shroud.

SCAFFOLDING

Forty edifices crowded
inside the gallery.

I have framed this portrait
with marble and gilt

    to grasp at the exact

        vanishing point.

A smoky river-fog
diminution of selves

    murmured off my skin.

Each direction
I swiveled my head—

mountain vistas and cedar-stacked

points of convergence

    vied for prominence.

All paintings, all frescoes,
every illuminated manuscript

with vignettes of divinity
crowded to the margins,

even living wills,
last wishes, hospital
discharge papers

promising cessation
of all interventions

    are mundane glimpses

        of annunciation.

Fliting on stout linen pulp,
fixed to mannerly vellum,
or inked on rock walls—

    heaven and hell
    are only pictures on earth.

A pen was folded
into my fingers;

plaster and tape
crackled with the bending.

    I was asked to sign and did.

ADORNMENT

PICC line jangling
at my throat—
        trade silver gorget askew.

Slim-gauge needles
navigate shallow shales
of the periodic table,
facsimiles for the benefit
of pitchy blood.

Twenty-five
moon-spun reels,
salted ground metals
churn gutward,
silken evening soles
consumed to slick
ruddy shreds.

Each flood noted
in a miniscule hand.

Ink gluts
on the freshets
of my thistle pulses;
follow down the cavern,
weight the vessel.
        Survey the dry land.

PASSING THE FRONTIER

Terra esonis incognita is a phrase used in cartography to indicate an unknown or imagined world. The etymology can break down in a few ways: land, secret, unknown; mythical hidden land; clouds on the borderland; across the border there is no life.

In 1887, the Dawes Severalty Act was passed under the presidency of Grover Cleveland as: "An act to provide for the allotment of lands in severalty to Indians on the various reservations, and to extend the protection of the laws of the United States and the Territories over the Indians, and for Other Purposes."

In a commissioner of Indian affairs report from the secretary of the interior, it was encouraged that Natives who resisted allotment or left their reservations should be "harassed and scourged without intermission" and made "as comfortable on" and "uncomfortable off" as conceivable. At the end of the report, there is a loose accounting of the numbers of Indigenous people divided into the following categories: civilized, semicivilized, wholly barbarous.

Allotment promised each head of family a grant of 160 acres to be held in trust by the U.S. government for twenty-five years. Agents were encouraged to urge allotments upon the tribes in any and every way possible. All around northeastern Indian Territory, registration for allotments was held out the back of a railroad caboose.

Obvious drivers of allotment include assimilation, white settlement, and resource extraction. Deeper in the dark river of the ink is permanent erasure of tribal lives and life: "It seems to me this is a self-acting machine that we have set going, and if we only run it on the track, it will work itself all out, and all these difficulties that have troubled my friend will pass away like snow in the spring time, and we will never know when they go; we will only know they are gone." So wrote Henry Laurens Dawes, Massachusetts senator, about his eponymous act.

Dawes was also an early proponent of national parks and was instrumental in having Yellowstone surveyed and appropriated. The removal of sacred sites was a paramount consideration to the success of the endeavor of allotment.

In 1889, Congress openly seized land in Indian Territory for white settlement. The land runs thundered. Many of the settler towns created in the land runs are ghost towns now. Timber, railroads, and mining leaving a host of cavernous emptiness in their wake. What is a ghost town in a nation whose settlements, roads, and parks are directly superimposed over Indigenous cities, trails, and sacred sites?

In America, the symbolic magic word for erasure is "first." I am weary of tasting the words as they leave my mouth. Turning frontiers of civilized and city and reservation and graft and outcome. Hours of scanning documents from 1833 or 1912 to make cruelties of syntax and word choice incriminate their drafters. The 1890s census report notes that all Shawnee Indians were fluent speakers of the language. The report itself was made possible by the Dawes Rolls that demanded each head of family be documented to receive an allotment. The rolls also tracked children and were instrumental in coercing families to cede their young to Indian boarding schools in the subsequent decades.

Of the Indian bills that became law in the forty-ninth and fiftieth sessions of Congress, six were railroad grants, in addition to the Dawes Act and the appropriation act. Property is often defined as "objectified will" in these documents.

The miles of railroad laid in that decade have not been exceeded since. The timber felled unimaginable. The invention of barbed wire was a boon for anyone with a taste for skin. Allotment was the whip and the balm, both delivered to the same hands. After the Dawes Act came the Curtis Act, eliminating judicial and executive aspects of tribal government, and then the Burke Act, which cemented a hierarchical government control of Indigenous people on allotments.

Miami, Oklahoma, was plotted from land bought from Ottawa tribal members and aggressively mined for lead and zinc. Railroad lines cut through individual allotments of the Shawnee, Miami, and Quapaw, and each tribal member received about a dollar and a half.

A dish with one spoon is ubiquitous in certain eras of American iconography. I sometimes find it stamped on very old artifacts in antique stores, especially around Ottawa County. The historical context of the dish and spoon is a visual symbol of all Indian land held in common.

Allotment tore some ninety million acres from tribes, but the scope is immeasurable in miles of land. Allotment created frontiers. The frontier of stolen land, stolen children, stolen memories. People are the storytellers, but the land is the memory palace. Allotment broke the trail into an impassable road from ancestors to progeny.

Severing these integrities takes a body and makes it a mined landscape. The breaking turns inward. Autoimmune illnesses occur when the body's protective systems curve upon themselves. For example, like many of my kin, my immunoglobin warriors became pulverizing machines and laid waste to the unity of my life's ecosystem, and I broke.

I was cautioned to expect a wait of three to four years for a transplant. The rate of dialysis morbidity at four years for a woman of my age, race, and diagnosis is around 60%. Wait time for organ transplants varies by region, blood type, and other medical factors.

Borders move land and time, and when you are waiting, the hours morph. Indigenous Americans are disproportionally impacted by the conditions that lead to loss of organ function and critically underserved by transplantation. Our lives are made short. When a patient does receive a graft, the system will fight it by way of the immune system even unto the death. There is no resolution to this form of severalty. The system is designed for integrity. An impulse to wholeness must be permanently suppressed. *Terra esonis incognita.*

In a sumptuous book of hours there are blank spaces
in the marginalia

where ghosts of the bear, lute player, and partridge
pencil a gray binary

between intent and completion. My hand shuffles
from the folio

of the *Prayer of One in Peril* to a sketch
of blue dent

corn mounds, to a tassel of bloody butcher just
above my head.

ADAGES

Faithful seekers whisper
civic mottos—rest
when you die, ask not
    the hour.

Great Father city's
venerable builders
measure avenues
with golden tape,

scribble equations
quantifying the span
of potential reverence
and anticipated profit.

These new cities are chartered
before they can be yanked
from their mothers.

Fresh earth shoveled
over the brined lapping
of estuary gates
    gushing pearls and tissue.

Forever sun—

four-chambered heart
thudding in a hot, bold sky;

the harder the wailing,
the harder the beating.

GREAT FOUNDER'S AXE

Early accounts of cedars
lining lower reaches

of the Cedar River estimate circumferences
of one hundred feet. The wood

is gone; the blade misremembered.
Who swings the axe to crack

wafers of such godly size?
First blows hew deep

fissures of erasure while the last
have yet to land.

Beg a timepiece
to pin down an analog

for the word *early*. Forgiveness
is to decision as a living tree is to decision

as mortality is to a good watch:
heavy in pocket, solid in hand.

EYE TURNED CROW

We have no true
    tragedy here—

the lecturer bemoans

American history's banality

while projecting a glossy photograph
of Berlin's monument
to burned books.

Slipping out the side door,
    my eye turns crow.

I've never seen book-burned violence—
charred edges of paper
    a murder of wings.

Running my hand
along moldering spines

is sometimes sufficient
to raven me

      into harried avarice.

Trace the indentions
of titles: flood paths
in the Nisqually Basin,

paperback print
of the *Dresden Codex*,

colophon of a sparrow
dimples a spine—
        history of child labor.

Corvids in flight and repose
decorate the walls
spouting whimsical chains
        of language.

When the workers

were placing the last
creamy bricks

along the crenels
of this library's
        gothic façade,

antipotlatch laws
allowed agents
to enter the ceremony,

seize artifacts,
make arrests,

cast narratives
upon the fire.

Crows follow wolves
who break open carcasses,

allowing the birds to feed—furtively,
I snatch a book from the cart,

crack its spine;
        halved to marrow.

BLACKFISH STATE

1.

My son points up to the
ship's name—the *Kaleetan*.

Arrow, I say
in Chinook.

A breeze tweezes a flight
of my hair with his,

so tonally similar
our locks

are inseparable—
murky raspberry brunette

in the softly drunken
beforehand light.

2.

As a child, I dipped
into the cove
on a dare.

     Dumbstruck—
cold water in my ears,
blanket of silt resting on starfish
so thick on the rocks.

I balanced myself
with two fingers
on a bright magenta tentacle.

Shivering up the beach,
I lobbed a dirt clod
at a faded church billboard
asking me if I had
     a God-shaped hole.

There was a pod of orcas
visible from the ship,
rippling neat and frisky
as a row of dominos
toppling in perfect order.

The woman next to me
gripped the guardrail
with such frenetic thrill
her false fingernails
popped off one by one.
     A bright coral ellipsis
     gliding into the wake.

Sleek hole inside me,
moving in the shape
of a blackfish.

3.

One hand to steady
the mild June currents underfoot,
it feels off to clasp my son
with my hand to my left hip,
but my right abdomen
is a swollen coil of surgical tubing.

I shade his forehead from the rain
with a brochure
for a bed and breakfast
and register
the avid track of his eyes
taking in the water's blurred end line,
the flicker of recognition
at the island's
          humpbacked breech.

If I were a person in a different place in time,
I would be known

by my city. I would broadcast seeds
by hand.

I would fragment corn with long poles
under the sounds

of the bobwhite and the nightjar, beyond
the hours. Untranslatable.

TROMPE L'OEIL

On a field trip
during my first year of teaching

I was hiking with students
between two cedar-spiked sea stacks

near Neah Bay. An orca's
black-and-white silhouette

sashayed across the waves,
young and frisky as a toddler in bathwater.

I was young. I thought
I'd captured

the essence of my calling,
climbing through an ecosystem

to the subtle prize of several souls
turned at the same angle

to observe a miracle
of whale skin erudition.

My aunt encouraged me to be a teacher
after I taught my cousin

to write her name. In my family
there were stories

of the boarding schools,
which baffled me. How my great-

aunts would rinse the littlest
girls' soiled sheets out before

dawn and switch the bedding
so that the older girls

tossed through the cold
dawns in clammy nests

while the little ones slept dry
on their traded sheets.

No one was ever caught.
How they adored the sewing circles

and never lost their ornate cursive handwriting.
Always hide trouble from the young.

Breaking down my classroom,
the last year I taught school—

I was so depleted. I bled through
shirts and once fainted from

anemia in the staff lounge.
I found a picture

tumbled in a storage closet
next to old seating charts,

primary-bright reward stickers,
a stale granola bar: faces locked

in astonishment, blazing
bright grins at the lens,

the subtitle *having sighted*
a killer whale, June,

written on the back
in a student's looping cursive.

QUARTER STRAIN

I.

First quarter
strain is the hardest.

Rust-font tributaries
dance in the margin
of the galley print textbook.
September's lecture
on comprehensive
learning standards

      sends me roving.

Glasses frame windows,
windows frame listing cedars.
"Ozymandias" in broadside hangs
by one staple
next to the definition of the doggerel:

      They went to sea in a Sieve, they did,
      In a Sieve they went to sea.

Shards of eraser—
steampunk spiders
prickly with embedded staples
cling to the ceiling panels.

My eyes drop
like cannonballs
in a mutiny.
Frank red bursts
groping for my spine,

shrill vermillion shrieks.

Little red mouths
	start chanting inside me.

2.

Afternoons dope me.

Sprawled on the floor,
        I wake covered and corralled
by cratered Lego fortresses,
scented markers plugged end to end,
Matchbox cars and fire trucks
in the chaotic parking patterns
        of emergency.

My son is prodding me
to greet him. *Say hello.*

Say it in Spanish.

Say it again in Tewa. Say it

        in Shawnee.

3.

The surgeon
writes my next act
with a lilac, felt-tipped pen
so that, as I am unconscious,
  she perforates
  her own name first.

Then my abdomen
in four careful slits.

Failed anesthesia,
panicked by the breathing tube,
thrashing on the table,
bile and blood aspirate
and rot in my lungs.

In postoperative pneumonia
I return to work,

one day teaching
the myth of Phaëthon,
Icarus and Daedalus,
Coyote and the Stars,
the story of a trickster
who lifts a whale
  from the lapping waves.

4.

I agonized for years
over my quartered self,
but the body
breaks whole.

Even so, I end
the year in thrall
to that trickster
of symmetry—
in the propitious
three out of four
survivors.

The deepest wound
bleeds steadily
around the surgical tube,
a long-stemmed dahlia
blooming at my side
through all four seasons.

OBELISKS IN THE CITY SQUARES

Haunt me with the negation
　　of obscured villages.

I am obliged
　　to read each plaque

etched on brass in a scrimmage
　　of anticipatory dread:

1800 and anything, the *heroic dead*
　　fallen in various battles, nothing

but savages and wild beasts, this place.
　　Obelisks as nouns and verbs

demand approach—colonial rebukes
　　to lure the very

water from my fingertips
　　with parsimonious concrete

or monolithic rock. Marble
　　is forever—bloodless

plinths puncture the blue over
　　threadbare towns.

American obelisks imbued with
　　belligerent fertility

and futility, when girdled
　　in chain or rope, convene

with gravity more easily
　　than was once imagined.

↓

Swales of salmonberry and arabesques
of sword fern

punctuate the coming of the warm season.
Balustrades of rain

and naked gray clouds trailing their fat feet
into summer

are broken when a heat dome blisters
shingles of orange

drought across the green needles of cedars.
Dentalia on the coast

boil in their own shells. Vines of beans explode
in lavender blossoms.

FIESTAS DE SANTA FE

There is a record

in a remote
Indian Health Service
filing cabinet

should proof
be required
for oneself or others.

The doctor
held and rotated an arm
in the gloved fingers
of his left hand
        just a bit aloft
        to check for breaks.

Looking back at the nurse
he murmured,
She doesn't
look much Indian—

with one finger probing
below the patient's
fattening right eye,

mopping honeysuckle-pink fronds
seeping from the cornea
with a two-by-two—
        except for this part.

As he flicked
the blue glove
and rusty squares of gauze
into the trash—

festooned flatbeds,
tinseled floats,
horse trailers driven by men

dressed as conquistadores
shuddered down Cerrillos Road
bound for the entrada.

CENTAUR CULTURE

I.

Grandfather was the only
rider never thrown
by a boxy Umatilla Hills pinto
    called Muffled Screams.

Between rodeos
he laid metal tracks
coast to prairie—shod hooves,
shovels, picks, gandy poles.

In the generation of his birth,

railroad seamed
American land
at a rate per capita
    that has yet to be exceeded
        in recorded history.

Starting to rise
back up before
his back hit dust: an artifact
    of ancestry.

2.

Before her body took a bad fall,
cousin said our kind

were natural riders.
She was a consummate
teller of thorny tales.

Later she said the cure
to her disease would turn
her hide to iron horse dusk.

I have a hard time
recollecting the exact shade
of her eyes,
but her red curls
         stay with me.

She could stick
to the spine of any horse,
but she didn't want to live
on those machines
         so she didn't.

Like green-broke
horses, we sunfish,
butterfly, crow hop—
we wear out our backs
trying to cast
         the burden.

3.

A half-remembered
elder taught me to pull
a rope against a winch
up to five pounds of pressure—a good rider
        never pulls harder.

As a kid I had
a lazy habit

looping the reins
around my fingers like macramé
until a hard buck

delivered me to gravity—
leather twisted into a tourniquet
        across my palms.

Withers and saddle horn
punching twisted horizons
        of sky and arena grime.

Never learning
but the hard way,
riding or thrown
from a little Appaloosa
or holding to the machines.

I had to trust the knot
        across my palms.

STRATA

My own folks
rode two horses
up a valley road
beside the Snoqualmie River,
syncline arches buried
under the layers of
second-growth cedar.
Crunching sword
ferns under hoof,
bridle deep in grasses
on a warm Sunday afternoon,
they tied the horses to cedars
and decided to settle
there on the mountainside.
Before all that,
sometime between
Shawnee Reservation
and Hanford Nuclear Reservation,
my grandfather would
ride mares over Satus Creek
into the farm where he worked
training quarter horses,
breed them to a foundation stallion
when the owner was gone,
and pocket the stud fee.
Horse Heaven Hills—
across the buckskin
anticline waves
of the Wallula Gap,
whole valleys carpeted
with sorrel yearlings would grow
into prize-cutting horses
becoming a kind

of family legacy.
I have a family story
that after the allotment act
one of my distant great-uncles,
refusing to sign
in the place
of a missing father,
was beaten so hard
he ran off
in the gloaming
bleeding a dark saddle pad
across the withers
of the fastest horse
in the barn.
In court papers, the horse,
a leggy red,
was considered adequate
compensation for the last
of the land
in its entirety.

Erasure is a trick. Surely the hours
have always shifted.

Golden eagles in the watershed:
a metaphor

for improbability so far north
or perhaps

a heraldry of the warming skies.
Kokanee salmon

run contrary to the named moon.
Seedy russet

sweetness of thimbleberries
a month too early.

Fledgling crows peel the peas
from their shoots

in their hunger. Each tassel of the corn
is a ladder to the kernel—

silken umbilical cords in the southern breeze.
Lay a skillet under the bed

to call a girl child to your garden,
a sickle for your boy.

CROSS-STITCH PRIMER

*"Because the words are necessary, they are included. Because the words
are inaccurate, they are struck through."*

—ARTHUR SZE

I am a new mother walking with my son strapped to my chest in the
cool rooms of the Museum of International Folk Art in Santa Fe. A wall
of primers is exhibited and the placard notes that firstborn girls were
encouraged to stitch an alphabet primer upon the death of a mother. A
method designed to grieve and honor her memory and provide practice for
the sewing work that would inevitably come.

A as ox—beast of burden dominating cool earth on sound hooves and
clean-boned forelegs. When the letters come to me like alchemy, A is the
beast that eats from my open palm with a velvet muzzle. B is the house
itself, not stick-built but flesh. Pregnant B, the woman with a belly and
swollen face like a lopsided chain-link. C carries water in its curves. Plunge
a hand into desert sand and grasp the C that was pictograph for camel until
time stripped it to essence. Slow curve of C on creamy linen press makes
me weak with desire, an ache in wrist and canine teeth no wet swallow can
soothe.

D is a soft threshold—crinkled sigh of the opened door's invitation and
supplication. E is the eye and it holds the burden of beholding. Imposing
the letter E summons a best friend from childhood. He was always getting
scolded for turning in papers without his name written on the line, so I was
always swooping in behind him correcting in careful lettering. Uppercase E,
I would write, and it was for the big eye of love.

F is the hitch sneaking out to rend—a whisper of nail sunk into wall. Flee
murmurs F into curved ear. The shadows of two long fingers and a thumb
leave their warped blue F on my upper arm. Straight and curved brackets
burdening a firstborn girl: G as soft gasp of a waterlogged door shutting
behind; H as clean-hewn fence. At eight I learned how to open and close a

fence from horseback, and since then the sound of a penciled H holds the aural satisfaction of the hiss of draped chain and spin of a lock shut firmly after the last weary chore. I is the body dead tired. I, my body stretched, wondering if it lies down in bed or grave.

J and K are the hand and palm. My elegant hand was born from studying a long, lean J on the page of an old hymnal with avid intent. L stands unimpeachable, an upright woman with long sword hidden in the grass. If I sign off on a letter with nothing but L, my blade is yours.

M is the water and N the fish—salty letters of home. Salmon flash pink and ocher like fallen leaves in the whipping high tide of the river, to which I fell asleep hearing. O is the wide-open eye, the serviceberries on the bush. Know them by what they see. P is the girl's head bobbing above the river's churning surface, one long leg kicking for the bottom mud.

Q is the needle's threaded eye. Once, in early love, I was asked my deepest secret. My roving mind was the oxygen-puffed cheeks on the round head of R and a long probing tremor ran through me like ink rippling down the funnel of a fountain pen. I think I'll die young. When I drop an R onto the page my pulse quickens, and I warn the white space to brace for blood.

S is the shadow of teeth and tongue in the body made horizontal by sleep or desire. The slack mouth open to the serpentine of slick shadow around white teeth. T is the mark to delineate sky from earth—finally a game I can win each time.

U is time's gentle softening of anther century's crisp V stitch of thread through cloth—the literature of my matriarchs. I study faded needlework primers with a troubled mind—a stitched alphabet as the recommended aid in grief for firstborn daughters upon the loss of a mother. My own stitches are as many and varied as any primer. They crimp my skin in a wavy persimmon U and V and W like faded madder root thread.

X nails the cross boards to the door for support. X this memory. I ran with a pack of cousins and neighbors at my aunt's house on the reservation. There were tunnels for a playground. The boys propped the openings with crisscrossed twigs. Is it true that a child was lost to a cave-in, or did I only hear of it and conflate the stories? I dream of a boy wearing a suit made of shale, Xs for eyes.

Y is the corn tassel in a gentle wind; anachronistic whisper of yonder in my mind. Z is the sickle, blade of sustenance to reap the crop and weapon in a pinch. Once in the field, Z whistled above my crown. I thought I'd be sliced in half. I impose Z in a tight flourish across the page, precarious ink edge of survival.

CRYPTIC CLICKS

Giddy with his new discovery
of measurement, my son dips

a discarded plastic zip tie into the water.
He drags a diamond into the sand

with his heel, surveys the receding tide
in a frenzy, then shucks his shoes

to climb the silver fluke of a scuffed statue.
Two women near the swings

sip coffee and squint into the horizon
as they debate the Indian Child Welfare Act.

J Pod is sometimes sighted
in the deep channel off Alki Beach,

speaking a language, scientists hypothesize,
unique unto itself. The smallest

of the two women tugs at her top and shivers,
latching an infant to her breast.

Chilled and tired, my son
raises his arms to be carried.

Like me, my boy
tends to follow statements

with a laid-back affirmative.
Northwestern: *You know what I mean?*

After his birth, I pumped milk
all through the early mornings

with one frenzied eye
to the nature documentaries on Nova.

Scratchy footage from the year of my birth
showed marine park employees

catching juvenile whales in the Salish Sea.
My own output was meager and lavender skim.

One time in ten, I poured straight into the bottle,
plastic liner forgotten. Milk splashing weakly

across the countertop, rendering unnecessary
the breast pump's preprogrammed synthetic wail.

When I was small, my mom once confessed
her great wish to jump from the back of a ferry

and swim back to her childhood
vacation home on Orcas Island.

My finger traced the white spots
on a killer whale key chain

as she talked, stunned by her audacity
to yearn for anything but me.

Camas glimpsed from a standing angle—
a flooded meadow.

Pockets of blue against the dull grasses.
Near Lacamas Grove,

the river's fork is confined by levees.
Large rock outcroppings

like treated vellum are scored with the striations
of glacial scour.

The tracts where camas was propagated
weeded and rebulbed

are under the shifted river. Thus, it is taken
as fact by those

who shifted the water that the tending
never occurred.

GORING A MAP

Bless the hands of the surgeons and make skilled their work.

    Washing one's hands of a problem

        conjures the image of Pilate

washing his hands as Jesus is turned over

    to be crucified. Occasionally I remember

        being made to wash my hands

in front of a nurse at a dialysis unit.

    She stood at my shoulder and checked

        my name off a list as I parted the lather

in a prescribed pattern. Something in me

    rinsed down the drain. The human hand is a universal

        symbol of agency. To conceptualize

living space on a map, accordion the paper.

    Slice elliptical spears,

        stretch them, let the cuts

articulate to symmetrical points—

    necessary severing of all tactile senses

        into flat gaze. A hand of glory

was severed from the punished,

    dipped in oil,

        and is believed to open any door.

A hand drafted the treaty

    and gripped the quill that signed it, and another

        hand hovered over the cursor to examine the signature.

I cover my son's hand with mine

    as he makes a map for school.

        North is a newer cartographic concept.

He struggles with the cursive letters

    of the directions on the wind rose.

        I commandeer the pencil like a benign breeze.

On a medieval map,

    God appears from the blue sky

        in the form of a disembodied hand.

REFUSAL OF THE RETURN

Palm-scattered
immunosuppressant ovals
and chalky steroids

like dispossessed seedpods
tickle a memory of the aural
hum of childhood sleep

when I might hear
river rush in my right ear
(Burntboot Creek, forked

from the Snoqualmie River),
susurrus of waterfall
in my left.

Austere and ascetic nomenclature:
Lindeman crossing into Buck,
North Fork Railroad Trestle,

Rattlesnake Lake,
Joseph, Judith, Seneca, Astrid.
Star women ambling

homeward without much quarrel,
never begging for cold water.
Salt or skin or iodine;

meager slivers of apotheosis.
Tokul—darkest water,
utterly still.

BIRD'S-EYE VIEW

The elevation
of a bird's-eye view

teases objective capacity.

Deep within
the Tolt's eastern tributary

something shuffles across a glade,

so massive and ungainly
my first intuition

       whispers young bear,

but then the wingspan
unfurls, copper and sorrel and ocher

      serrated chalcedony—vast.

Vast and dignified,
a golden eagle

is improbable
this far north.

These birds are known
      to bring down young deer.

Bald eagles circle
most days, though

when I was a child
they were so rare

school stopped one day
so we could all walk

      to the river and watch
      as one lit upon oak's crown.

Two perspectives
      glide within:

Each day, over crossed

by birds of consequence—

eagles, hawks, snow geese, swans

      I am beheld.

Each day I walk

until over crossed

      by birds of consequence

I am beholden.

Beak and talon,
mahogany-tip feathers

against the hazel haze
      of mist and grass.

Objectivity—
      the wind this wing

        will cut.

←——————

Northern Spy apple trees grow
crooked and gray

from cores lobbed out of train windows
near trestles

over the Snoqualmie River.
The hands that

flung them from windows dodged
felled cedars.

Each path an enigmatic mosaic
verged in coal:

Gardens of mermaids and graylings and mares.
Cawing birds

of knowledge and recollection.
Hustling down

an abandoned logging road into a slough—
heron vectors cloud bank.

HER PACES

Under tree canopy
I skitter away

from a curious deer,
shooing it up mountain.

I can't shake
a hunger to ask

about all the missing women.
My cousin, for one.

Gone for more than a week,
then appeared sunburnt

but talkative along the banks
of the Wenatchee River.

How many deer did she
amble past? Everyone so glad

to see her homebound
we didn't ask

how she spent that week.
Up and down slim gorges,

I've started to trace creeks
so deep into the forest

I tumble out the side
of a mountain

in a different valley
five miles distant

from the city where I started.
It is unwise to admit

to these odd affinities: talking
to a deer for one, absconding

untethered for another
while my relatives

are plucked so often
from the terrain.

I'm pacing a theory—
only after penetrating

past all indications,
mauve flash of brush-footed moth,

downy waft of rut rippling
off a deer-rubbed tree,

I register the slight velvet fibers
of antler down and vanish.

FREEHOLD TERRITORY

Seventh room, seventh floor.
A squatter on contested territory
holding fluid in my lungs
like a phantom daughter.
To come forth once more
from the opened torso
to navigation stars,
boundary line sprinting.
Lazarus. Lazarus. Lazarus.
I badly long for the beckoning,
but the fee is never simple.

THE NECK VERSE

Madrona skin twists
to red ribbons
along suburban flanks.

Old scars only seem
unforgettably garish
until the fresh ones settle in.

Girdling cancers of black rot
harry trunks,
hastened by the heat

of human traffic.
With age, this species
develops a desperate

need for sunlight.
It takes time and agonizing
necessity to become gregarious

at the crown. A juvenile stand
hewn by the footpath is beaten
too bloody to metaphor,

green skinned and beyond all help.
Impossible to read, resistant
to lyricism, consider

the human riddle of the neck verse.
Recitation of Psalm 51
was once considered

sufficient reason to spare

a certain class of soul
from the noose.

Precontact trees, utterly
unique to the Pacific coast,
madronas will cling, salt whipped,

to ocean ledges for decades,
but transplant a west-facing sapling
to an eastern bluff and there it ends.

Squash leaves welt my forearms and ankles.
Water runnels trail

through the dirt on my shins.
All the star women

came back home without much fuss.
I strip the beans

from their shells. A deep purple
like trade beads.

Perpetual life inside each seed makes the etymology
animate in Shawnee, static in English.

DOCTRINE OF SIGNATURES

Like a figure
from an illuminated manuscript,

fingers elongated,
richly robed,
wide, unfocused eyes,

toes pointed down as if bedbound,

lion at my feet,
ox over my shoulder,
bear in my belly.

> In this place
> I aestheticize meadow
> and anesthetize current.

Grisaille of lungwort lichen
jockeys branches and boulders
across the ghost town.

On the cusp of
the flood meadow—

> a hop shed sweating
> hundred-year creosote.

To the west,
under the schoolhouse—
> the foundation
> of the longhouse.

In stock storytelling convention,
the revenant hero

upon fulfillment
of a divine purpose
draws a promise—

    Next time, let me go to my rest.

Canopy of lichen,
cousin to the wolf poisoner,
expectorant, binder of medieval perfumes.

If the three-kingdom city
of algae, fungi, and yeast
is never divided
into a severalty of parts,
lichen may live forever
in misty seasonality.

Cover my eyes with
flat river stones
that remember
the press of canoes.
Open my lips.
Fold the molting world
under my tongue.

    Next time, let me lichen.

GROUND LAPIS

Worthy occasions
    divide time by tense.

In my language

the word *when*

is expressed
as a place in time—

sky door to the personal

    invention of perspective.

When my son
was only just walking,

he watched dancers.

    A small figure
    within the abiding ceremony,

    he stood, moved in drummed
        time and rhythm,
            extended his arms.

I was so moved,
I had to look away.

Ground-lapis desert sky
drank my eye and left

    that image branded in sanctified blue.

In one place in time,
a docent rambled
        about angles of proportion

in a tiny chapel.

I cast my arm against sunbeams

filtering through the tops
of lancet windows

        as if I were sheltering from a blow.

In a fresco of the court of heaven—

Mercy sits to the right.

The quotidian agonies
of death are rendered
small and faint.

To say I will remember

        to the end of my days
        begs a portrait.

Small eagle dancer
within the abiding ceremony
        moving arms wide
                to mimic wingspan.

Memory is a fresco.

        Give your eye to the sapphire.

RIVER CITY

Grasping for the home sense
of the river city, I become
increasingly enthralled
with the heavenly city

ticking inside the clock's
lavish precincts. Hours I did not
count on becoming
the river home I long for.

Flood of settlement
subsuming the divine cities—
our rivers exiled by their rivers,
christened bucolic, baptized

for dead fathers, but not ours.
Trinity gates for each
cardinal direction draft
the divine city's parameters.

City contingent on river;
beneath the dim crust of exile,
foundation stones laid
with sapphires glisten

alongside rivers buried under soybean
and wheat. No word for *burial*
on the river's faceted tongue
in the city where I stay.

Close my mouth so the spider
weaving between

fronds of preacher beans and fence posts
may not count

my teeth. The inchworm does not pause
to measure me

for my coffin. You see the shape of the land
more clearly for its austerity.

For these many years
I have held

a note at the end of my files:
Patient must mourn

the death of her old life and accept
limitations. Beseech

an abandoned orchard of trees
whipped bare,

anemic, bilious, and green skinned,
listing against

a logged sidling's last fringe,
about the banalities

of the cuts, while tying a rag of supplication
to the lowest

branches, and blissfully, they
hold silence.

WHY LAZARUS

Because a woman was disinherited
    by a disinterested witness
    in Turkey Ford, Oklahoma,
    because she married
    in the Indian way
    and zinc was found
    on her allotment.

For the sake of the sixth-born child.
    Last of the animal surname,
    son of he named
    for the third son
    of Jacob and Leah,
    who ran from home chased
    by a flickering length of leather.
    Like a contrary land breeze
    from mountain to sea,
    not stopping until he
    hit salt water.

Because my own father's father
    was made citizen
    at age fourteen. Beneath the land
    he tended for his children,
    covered rivers flow
    under suburban foundations.

Because a park, reservation, or monument bears the same official
    symbol on the map:

Park, reservation, or monument   _____ · _____

    A lonely figure surrounded by endless fields.

Because in removal,
the Shawnee were not permitted
        to carry any tools
        that could be used
        as weapons.

So Lazarus broke ground
        with his fists and toes, raked red earth
        with a gar's jaw. Peeled limbs
        from the trees to burn for warmth,
        slid corn kernels down the side
        of his forearm into holes
        quarried with his bare hands.

Because the cougars extirpated
        from Shawnee homelands
        track me in my sleep
        and a knot in a tale
        shows that the story could go either way.

For the sake of the words of faith:
        no talk, instruction, or translation
        in native language was permitted
        to the daughters of Lazarus
        at the Seneca Indian School,
        even for the youngest pupils.
        The Shawnee Bible
        being the only exception.

Because an ancestor was the twelfth
        child of that year
        and the missionaries
        tallied the twelfth letter
        of the alphabet
        and went thumbing
        through the Bible for a name.

Because the etymology
  of the word *martyr* is to bear witness:
  Indian trails holding steady
  under concrete highways.

Because Lazarus made Jesus weep
  as a friend and called him
  back to the world.

For we, the resurrected,
  so solitary in our vast fields,
  need to call out to one another
  by name in this new territory
  where the fee simple is neither.

THE MEADOW

All these events have
already taken place,

and but for the mountain pass
with its attenuation

of the ravenous
hungers of migration,

and the fur wars' fevered
appetites for skin, this was

a place of boundless plenty.
And the inhabitants lived

in abundance here,
girded by the protective trident

of the many-forked
river. And at that time

the river was the great
street, clear and strong,

as that of the heavenly city.
And the past in this view

is a book to study well
and quote from memory,

but an object to be unhanded
at will. And in this past

they came as thieves
up the river

in a flotilla of fifteen canoes.
Above the meadow

across the trident-scored mountain
the rams ran up taluses

to caves upon the sounding
of the trumpet, smell

of the flood on their horns.
And liberties were taken

across the meadow.
One fort was crafted

of unpeeled hemlock,
another of long, slender

fir poles. And each generation's
rough courtship seeded the meadow,

unions jostling underfoot
in fecund thrall to the

grassy overcovering.
And the mosses and lichen

cycled in perpetual resurrection.
And sickles thrust

into the land beckoned forth
orderly rows. Forts

became farms. Schools and lyceums
and territorial post offices

were built over the longhouses.
And women were taken

for a decade or two.
Some survivors were returned

with their children
upon statehood proclamation.

And some of the begotten
did indeed possess the cities

of their enemies as promised
in Genesis, but this was long

ago, and they were people
of their time. And all

accounts to be taken
as such. To wit, in a

slim book bound
with oxblood leather,

seven pages from this time
are devoted to the accidental

shooting of a cow
on the western edge

of the meadow and
speculation that the soldiers

may have done it intentionally
for desire of any meat

but venison. All those
mobilized on the meadow being

men of their age
and thus crack shots.

And a sparse two
sentences are allotted

to the Natives
who were shot from the banks

of the river for sport
from the leeward door

of the territorial fort
that opened to the water

on the edge of the meadow
in that time out of mind.

2. THE SYMBOLIC HISTORY VIEW

When skirted by a river's confluence,
>   a mountain range, or other natural boundary,
>   a meadow is an optimal gathering place; lush cradle
>   with its own established treaty rites
>   of diplomacy and abundance.

The word *meadow*'s English etymology
>   precedes the dissolution of the monasteries
>   and the routine cadastral measurement of land.
>   So it leaves a soft cast in the throat,
>   a taste of Edenic green in its syllables.

Meadow is a woven basket
>   pressed under epochal currents
>   reaping old arrows of hunger,
>   sifting hard mineral traces of appetite.

Many perceive heaven
>   in the form of a meadow. The path of righteousness
>   is carpeted with violet flowers. The open
>   field symbolizes doctrine; faith is grasses.

3. THE PROPHETIC FUTURE VIEW

Each side of the promised city stretches 1380 miles long,
but even this lordly perimeter could never bind the hungers

of the nations of appetite. Walls of jasper, plated streets of gold,
foundation stones of chalcedony and sapphire. In a rupture

of violence, the first town destroyer proclaimed: *God made
me the messenger of the new heaven and the new earth*

*of which he spoke in the Apocalypse. And he showed me the spot
where to find it.* Rapture apotheosis requires this: grasses seeded

with blood to ride over bridle deep, proclaiming the hour has come.
Men will not be held by the heavenly city with meadows to burn.

4. THE CONTINUOUS HISTORY VIEW

We stand well inside a fraction of the prescribed millennium. Look diligently for clues, historicist. This is your great-great grandfather we are talking about. His axe may yet hang in some standing valley barn. You may be the namesake when the time for the accounting comes.

In order of appearance from the skin down to the marrow, the meadow may be classified: river flood sediment, glacial till, glacial outwash, bedrock. A glacial dam broke and a lake of water pressed its damp tread into the valley. Rivers and sloughs and creeks caressing the meadow from all sides tend to exhibit a braided morphology, which is to say you can expect to scrabble over large rocks on one side of the river and dip your toes in smooth silt climbing out the other.

Presently, the lacy amethyst froth of blooming camas from the time of *Lacamas Field* is rarely seen in the meadow but could return, may be replanted in the next years depending upon intent and climate. The river otters, once plentiful, now rare, are sometimes noted far up the river tributaries, teeth bared for the salmon runs. It makes the wars hard to talk about. So now when someone finds a cannonball from 1855, it is an artifact of dense mythology to prod. There were forts and blockades made in haste, and the meadow was selected, was considered most defensible, and was called *Ranger's Prairie*.

For a few decades, the world's largest hop farm was here. Workers were separated by race then tribe and were called each season to *The Greenchop Field*, and numbered brass plates were issued to be worn around the neck until surrendered at any of the toll gates posted on all access points of the river's forks. The wide green lozenge of the meadow was netted in a sturdy fence, later repurposed for the *Meadowbrook Dairies* of the last four generations, posts still visible from the walking trails today.

When I was young, I asked my folks: Why do we live here? Why this valley meadow?

We liked it. We desired it. We went out riding one day. And it enchanted us.
Even now, I walk over this meadow in the place I think of as my home-
town, knowing all this, beholding the land,
spread before the mountain like a looted emerald. If pressed, I would paint
the icon of heaven in these shades of green.

5. THE SWORD VIEW

A gang of fifty elk saunter
the leeward edge as one body,
the last of the light hemming
across mountain crowns.

The elk press, slow and deliberate,
until the meadow is defined,
a rippling frontier
between their calves
hidden in the marsh grass
and me, walking slowly backward,
pulses thudding across
the ridges of my fists.

> To conceptualize the words
> of faith, I was taught to
> hold a phantom sword
> in my hand and study the verses
> by its points.

> An allegory of conquest
> so simple a child
> can understand it.

> *Is there a sin to avoid?*
> *Is there a promise to believe?*
> *Is there an example to follow?*
> *Is there a command to obey?*

I am too close and have forgotten
that I am a stranger here.
Ocher ripples of hair
crest on the nearest elk.

The crown of my head
is the blade tip pointing
to the dark opal of sky:
What can be inferred about the divine?

LAND BEYOND MAP

Here the river is the color of a moss agate frothing to vellum at the currents. Strata of lichen mark the waterline across the river rocks from dark coffee to otter pelt to spit-bug green to citrine at the crown. Smokey quartz and camas of the October sky in layers—water's delicacy and restraint as mist in the air and its ferocity and favor as liquid in the river.

Here, the most pitiless form of exile is thirst, and it is held at a distance.

Here, a man came up water to the valley with a new hat, a new suit, a green broke horse, and squeaking leather traces and insisted his name upon the place. Bullets embedded in the trees sleep deep under the mantle of maiden fern. Canoes were overburdened with old growth, coal was slivered from the mountains, and lumber skids to the water became front yards.

Here is the sting of rumination. Nettles are a sure sign of human habitation—they love our wake of phosphate. Who am I to love my hometown when I don't even know how to call it by its own name? In Isaiah, the heavenly city is set in stones of antimony and laid with foundations of sapphire. I only trust the maps whose edges hint at the outer boundaries of heaven and whose cardinal directions are marked in barite, marine shells, copper, and horseshoes.

Here in the time of the wilted lunar cycle: *Ha koowesilaasamamo?* How are you breathing now? Salmon in the river curve like pale reflections of the crescent moon.

Here selves spawn and sway—aspirations and obligations needling through the pale stitches of my skin.

Here beside a deserted rodeo arena, the Snoqualmie River braces itself to cascade. A tiny hop shed breathes out hundred-year-old creosote fumes and splits the green skin of damp meadow like a rotten tooth.

Here in the gap of garish yellow devil's club, follow a deer trail down to the river and pass the plants that cure warts or hasten a purge to the trees that bend most readily into longbows. Sundogs cast three circles of deep light.

Here warriors dipped into the currents to cool their blood and slow their pulses as a prelude to returning home from the wars.

Here I used to run wild with a pair of siblings from the trailers across the road. We'd race three to a horse until dark. My little buckskin with a long crescent snip and dark dorsal stripe, we liked trotting her into the edge of the sand and then tumbling into the water. Sometimes I dream of my hands on the reins; I'm peeking between the black points of my mare's curved ears into the valley's cracked verdant geode of moss and lichen.

Here I walk away from the river and press my hands to the sides of the hop barn. Memory is a child's moon. There is no apparent when, just places in time. Each territory is a harvesting crescent scythe that severs the clock. Desired or rebuked, I dwell in and upon the recollecting cities as they ripen outside the hours and beyond the map—I am teeming with souls.

Here is the place in time that I leave the river on foot, as the evening turns the saturated meadow the darkest shade of lapis veined with the grazing silhouettes of elk. A pale is a border and I cross one, stepping from the fringe of red cedars to see once more the light of the stars dissolving the sapphire boundary.

BEAD WORKERS

Needles in skilled hands
pulled through cloth or skin
move of their own

gilded volition.

     Taaniwe laakwa?

In Shawnee,
you ask
     where in time

as opposed to when

and it helps me

     consider folds of territory,

tilled by memory and capacity
where the ones I tender
     bloom quietly and eternally.

A strain of heirloom corn
roughly translates to the word

sustainer—worlds

that germinate inside such a word:

wild horses, lilting shadows
glimpsed in the elbows of the hills

     like opaque flags of prayer.

My distant kin in Neosho

folded deep indigo beans
into the palm of my hand

and said try them

    where you stay.

Within the words of a blessing
in my husband's language

I recognize through repetition:

    The word for city.

    The word for garden.

Like an heirloom seed,

I was sown and cultivated
    back from the brink.

To rise within

    a place in time,

hands sorted
hundreds of seeds;
medicine and sustenance—

pallid disks of immunosuppressants
    and steroids.
    Flint corn from the Scioto Valley.

All those moments
I shook too hard

to do it myself.

Running a finger

across the slight backs
of trade beads: cornflower blue,

      grass green, the white-heart red
          a fire flood of sunset.

I feel the shadow
of my aunt's beading

wringing my neck and wrists.

Spells to protect

      my casing gates.

Cerrillos turquoise

      threaded into my earlobes.

Intricate blueprints

to the homelands
kept my toes
from the sky ladder's

      sapphire rungs.

Sustainers are all around:

songs chanted
seven states away—glistening exhalations

of devotion and sacrifice,

        migrations of breath.

Adorn the skin with glass.

In a place in time

the ground warms and opens—

the hour is right,

        stitch a seed and it sustains.

Upon my return I am mistaken
for a gardener,

sowing a verdant book of hours.
Swans trumpet

in bird falls of old logging ponds.
Snow geese

with black-tipped wings drip ink
down my fingers

when I twist into the rocky outcroppings
of the Snoqualmie Reach

looking for western hemlock
beyond the talus field.

A black-tipped tail flickers into the trailside brush,
a gunshot sounds close.

Honor the harvest—the opener of the blade
must close it.

ACKNOWLEDGMENTS

I would like to extend my gratitude to the editors and readers who welcomed poems, sometimes in earlier iterations, into literary spaces of story and image:

Anomly: "Why Lazarus"

Arc Poetry Magazine: "Fiestas de Santa Fe"

As/Us: "Cryptic Clicks"

Consequence: "The Meadow: Preterist View" and "The Meadow: Continuous History View"

Cutthroat: "Mistaken for a Gardener"

F(r)iction: "Watch Face"

Guesthouse: "Strata" and "Detasseling"

MOSS: "Blackfish State"

Pageboy: "Great Founder's Axe," "Obelisks in the City Squares," "Shawnee Word for Principal City," "Adages," and "Centaur Culture"

Poem-a-Day (Sherwin Bitsui): "Twelve Gates"

Poetry: "Beadworkers" and "The Meadow Views: Sword and Symbolic History"

Prairie Schooner: "Passing the Frontier"

River Mouth Review: "Her Paces"

Seattle Review of Books: "Refusal of the Return"

South Seattle Emerald: "The Neck Verse"

Split This Rock: "Freehold Territory"

Tahoma Literary Review: "Ground Lapis"

The City of Redmond: "Bird's Eye View"

The Massachusetts Review: "River City"

The Rumpus: "The Rhetorical Feminine" and "Adornment"

Tusculum Review: "Painterly"

Under a Warm Green Linden: "Beauty Screen," "Lacamas Canon," and "Cross Stitch Primer"

World Literature Today: "Moving Classrooms"

Yellow Medicine Review: "Goring a Map," "Scaffolding," and "Land Beyond Map"

Personal Best: Makers on Their Poems That Matter Most, edited by Erin Belieu and Carl Phillips, Copper Canyon Press, 2023: "River City"

Cascadia Field Guide: Art, Ecology, Poetry, edited by Elizabeth Bradfield, CMarie Fuhrman, and Derek Sheffield, Mountaineers Books, 2023: "Doctrine of Signatures"

Living Nations, Living Words, edited by Joy Harjo, Norton Press, 2021: "The Rhetorical Feminine"

Native Voices: Indigenous American Poetry, Craft and Conversations, edited by CMarie Fuhrman and Dean Rader, Tupelo Press, 2019: "Perspective (Invention of Perspective)" and "Eye Turned Crow"

New Poets of Native Nations, edited by Heid Erdrich, Graywolf Press, 2018: "Quarter Strain"

―――――――――――――

Bless my guides and caregivers: my husband, my son, my family, my colleagues, my students, my healers and donor, and my friends who are true and wise. There is no better luck than to share this place in time with these souls and to stand in the illumination of their light.

I would like to offer my gratitude to the communities that have welcomed me and assisted in the creation of this book: The Eastern Shawnee Tribe of Oklahoma, The Absentee Shawnee Tribe of Oklahoma, Seattle Arts and Lectures, Richard Hugo House, Tin House, Northwest

Native Writers Circle, Odle and Tyee Middle Schools, Hedgebrook, Artist Trust, 4Culture, The City of Redmond Poet Laureateship, The Poetry Foundation Poet Laureateship Fellowship, The Virginia Mason and Valley Medical Systems, Native Arts and Cultures Foundation, Jack Straw, and the King County Public Library System. *Niyaawe* to the Shawnee Tribal Language circle for words and guidance. Thanks to my extended family for their stories and shared memories.

ABOUT THE AUTHOR

Laura Da' is a poet and teacher. A lifetime resident of the Pacific Northwest, Da' studied creative writing at the University of Washington and The Institute of American Indian Arts. Da' is Eastern Shawnee. She is the author of *Tributaries*, winner of the American Book Award, and *Instruments of the True Measure*, winner of the Washington State Book Award. Da' lives near Renton with her husband and son.

Made in the USA
Coppell, TX
05 October 2025